Successful Termination

William J. Morin

A Division of Drake Beam Morin, Inc.
100 Park Avenue New York NY 10017
212 692-7700

Printed in the United States of America   ISBN 1-880030-06-3

Table of Contents

From the Author

Termination of a person, executive or non-executive, is not only a traumatic experience for the individual, but is also a tense act for the manager handling the termination. Moreover, it is a potentially hazardous situation for the organization.

Companies often ask, "What is the single most prevalent mistake that companies make when approaching the act of termination?" The simple answer to that question is, "Most companies approach terminations too emotionally."

In other words, a manager getting ready to terminate someone tends to get very emotional about it and wants to approach the termination too quickly. One example comes to mind. When the author was counseling a company about a planned termination, a manager kept asking if he could do the termination that day. With the help of the personnel officer and the author, the manager was persuaded to prepare to do the termination in a proper fashion a few days later. All too often, when preparing to terminate individuals or groups of individuals, corporations and managers have a tendency to move too quickly. We have observed the pain and havoc caused by haphazard termination: persons not knowing if they have or have not been terminated; persons left in a state of shock from which they never recover emotionally and/or spiritually. And yes, we have seen cases of suicide as a result of brutal and insensitive termination.

This booklet provides a planned and structured approach to the termination process while addressing the emotional impact as well. It is possible to minimize the trauma and protect the interest of all parties involved. Toward that end we are providing you with guidelines based on over twenty-five years of experience working with persons affected by corporate and organizational change.

Preface

othing endures but change. The truth of that statement is never more obvious than when one looks at the world of business, where the issues of this and future decades are issues of massive change. They include: globalization, emerging technology, changing markets, corporate mergers and acquisitions, quality initiatives, restructuring, and revitalization.

Central to the issue of corporate change is the judicious administration of human resource policy. Companies are struggling to realign human and technological resources in ways that will spell productivity and profit. The demands on corporate performance have increased and the pressure is felt all the way down at the level of the individual worker. Productivity and quality are translated into specific performance criteria. Specific job skills coupled with the more general requirements of flexibility and adaptability are considered more important than ever before. As a matter of survival, organizations are developing plans and defining strategies that emphasize performance and the bottom line, with less emphasis on an individual's years of service or loyalty to the organization. Employees at all levels are feeling the impact; gone are the days of "full employment" and "cradle to grave" security. Companies that have been models of stability are now in the midst of downsizing. The long-term bond that once united employee and company is a thing of the past.

From the company's standpoint, the decision to terminate an employee or a group of employees is fraught with emotional, legal, public relations, and business implications. From a personal perspective, terminations can be physically, emotionally, and financially devastating.

Is there a way to balance the needs of the organization and the employee? Is the concept of successful termination realistic? Experience has shown that the answer is a resounding "YES."

As with any decision that impacts human life and livelihood, there is a need to preserve dignity and self-esteem. From a business perspective, the decision to terminate must be carefully considered, thoughtfully planned, and skillfully conducted. Care must be taken to protect the interests of all parties: the terminated employee and his or her family, the manager who delivers the message, the remaining workers, and the company.

Successful termination means that the employee hears and understands the necessary information, knows what to do next, and retains his/her dignity and self-respect throughout the process. For the company, it means that all legal and ethical responsibilities have been fulfilled, that its internal and external images have been preserved, and any negative impact on the morale and productivity of remaining employees has been minimized. In essence, a successful termination is a thought out, sensitively conducted management act that minimizes trauma for the individual and the company.

In response to the magnitude of the issues and their effects on individuals and companies, a professional consulting industry called Career Transition Management has emerged. Drake Beam Morin, Inc. is the worldwide leader in providing Career Management Consulting. Whether or not your company uses the services of Drake Beam Morin, Inc. to assist you in individual or group terminations, this booklet is designed to guide you in your efforts toward successful termination procedures.

Introduction

Termination. Few words in our business vocabulary evoke as much fear and anxiety. These emotions are not felt only by the person(s) who will be terminated, but also, in almost equal measure, by you—the Manager responsible for delivering the termination notice.

Nothing in our formal business training prepares us for this task. Some important questions must be answered: What are the justified reasons for termination? What kinds of documentation do I need? What do I say? How do I say it? Where do I say it? When do I do it? What if he/she gets upset? We are overwhelmed by emotions that increase our anxiety as we hear ourselves saying:

> "I've worked with Jim for 20 years."

> "Jane's got two kids in college."

> "Harry's been with us from the beginning."

> "There must be a reason why he isn't cutting it; maybe we can give him another job."

> "They just bought a new house."

And we begin thinking:

> "Maybe I should have done more to help him."

> "This could happen to me someday."

> "What if she really gets angry at me?"

The act of termination is one of the most difficult and

demanding responsibilities of the Manager. It is one that requires discipline, sound business judgment, and sensitivity. In short, a manager must balance the needs of the individual with those of the organization.

This booklet is intended to help you resolve the myriad emotional and practical issues that are rooted in the word "termination." Its purpose is as follows:

> To help you understand your responsibilities as Manager during the termination process.

> To enable you to better balance the human needs of the terminated individual and the business needs of the company.

> To guide you through the critical steps of terminating an employee.

> To assist you in communicating termination information to remaining employees.

> To reduce trauma for you, the Manager, the individual affected and for the company.

Planning and Documentation

1

The responsibility for documenting and carrying out terminations rests with the Manager. It is he/she who monitors job performance and group productivity. Whether the termination is due to cause, job elimination, or poor performance, the Manager must identify the problem, take appropriate steps to correct it, support his/her efforts with documentation, and, when appropriate, convey the decision to the Employee. The Human Resources/Personnel Department can offer advice and counsel, but it is the Manager who must carry out the termination process.

There are basically three reasons for terminating an employee:

Cause: e.g., stealing, misrepresentation, unethical or dangerous behavior.

Job Elimination: e.g., going out of business, elimination of a business unit, merger, or adverse economic conditions.

Poor Performance: e.g., failure to attain agreed-upon goals, failure to master required skills, or failure to perform assigned tasks.

These reasons are often influenced by more subtle factors such as "poor chemistry" and "office politics." Nevertheless, a Manager who recommends terminating an employee should be able to document valid reasons for the decision. For example, the Manager must be able to show that "poor chemistry" does, in fact, affect this person's ability to perform his or her job.

Termination is a business decision and a professional management function. As such, it should be supported by sound reasoning, good judgment, and hard facts. It is essential to avoid the emotional knee-jerk reaction so often related to termination. The Manager who fails to plan the termination appropriately jeopardizes an individual's livelihood and creates great risk for the company. Individual employees are protected by law, and companies may be liable for the actions of managers who do not plan and conduct terminations appropriately. Because company policies differ, the Manager should work closely with the Human Resources Department before the termination and throughout the process. This is particularly true when termination results from cause or poor performance. Working with the company's Human Resources Department, the Manager should follow a systematic process of documentation that will substantiate management's complaints about an employee's behavior or performance.

When the decision to terminate results from performance issues, the Manager will be wise to rely heavily on the company's system for reviewing individual performance. Performance Appraisals that are periodically and carefully administered are one way to alert an employee of a potential termination. If the Employee does not correct the performance problem, the appraisal will serve to demonstrate that the Employee has been advised of performance deficiencies and has been given an opportunity to correct them. Termination for poor performance should not come as a shock to an employee. Usually documentation of written and verbal feedback for at least six months prior to termination should be considered essential to protect the interests of all parties.

When termination is the result of job elimination or large-scale reductions in force, the Manager should consult with policy-makers in order to clearly understand the rationale for the company's decision before communicating any information to the Employee. Various strategies can be used to determine which employees will have to leave the company. Forced ranking and seniority are only two possibilities. In addition, a voluntary separation component may reduce the number of involuntary terminations, particularly if incentives are offered.

Regardless of the reason for termination, a well-conceived and carefully implemented plan benefits all parties: the Employee, the Manager, and the company.

Specifically:

Employee trauma is minimized because the time, place, reasons for the termination, and next steps have all been coordinated to protect the Employee's dignity and self-esteem. In addition, questions and details that may be of concern to the Employee have been anticipated and responses prepared.

Manager anxiety is reduced because he/she has had time to analyze the facts of the situation, seek advice and counsel from Personnel or Human Resources professionals, organize the meeting agenda, anticipate reactions, and deal with his/her own emotions.

Company liability may be reduced because the documentation and the decision have been discussed and reviewed by appropriate levels of management. Plans for communicating the decision to other employees are in place, and, if appropriate, additional resources are available to assist the terminating Manager and the Employee.

Preparing for the Termination Meeting

2

Having documented the need for the termination, the next responsibility of the Manager is to prepare for the termination interview. This phase of the process includes: coordinating logistics, preparing materials, preparing the termination message, arranging next steps, and preparing himself/herself.

Coordinate Logistics

The Supervising Manager should conduct the termination alone. Some company policies require that a representative of Human Resources also be present although this can create a feeling of "two against one."

There is no good time for a termination interview; however, early in the week and early in the day are recommended times. This allows the Employee to come back with questions or begin outplacement immediately. Never terminate on a Friday when an employee faces a long weekend without the structure necessary to move on to next steps.

Be prepared for emergency situations that could arise (e.g., health-related problem) and have a list of emergency phone numbers at hand.

Prepare the logistics of transition: transfer projects or work assignments; clear Employee's office or work area; arrange for return of confidential data, identification, and keys.

Prepare Materials

Assemble written documentation if the termination is performance related.

If the termination is due to job elimination, explain the rationale.

Prepare all severance information in writing: notification letter (working and nonworking notice); salary continuation/severance period; benefits; outplacement counseling; and other pertinent information.

Prepare the Message

Write out the "script" you will use during the termination meeting and the information you will convey to remaining employees.

Try to list two or three factual reasons for the termination. Keep everything short and to the point.

Arrange Next Steps

Schedule additional meetings, e.g., Human Resources, Personnel, Outplacement.

Review what should be done with personal belongings. (This can be done by the Human Resources Department.)

Specify when Employee should say good-bye and leave premises.

Prepare Yourself Emotionally

Don't assume personal responsibility for the termination: it is a business decision based on business needs.

Prepare your approach and talk about your feelings with Human Resources professionals.

Acknowledge your anxiety and be sensitive to your feelings throughout the process.

Do not discuss your plans with associates and friends. This will avoid gossip and rumors before you are ready to conduct the termination meeting.

Anticipate Employee Reactions

Role-play or practice dealing with anticipated reactions, such as Shock, Anger, or Denial (see Chapter 3).

Comprehensive preparation will benefit you and the Employee by providing structure and objective information that will keep you focused in the midst of a difficult meeting.

Preparation Checklist

Coordinate Logistics:

☐ Human Resources notified and approvals received.

☐ Manager/Employee appointment scheduled.

☐ Emergency information on hand; physical problems identified.

☐ Outplacement firm identified.

☐ Logistics/transition of work responsibility arranged.

☐ Security check-out arranged.

Prepare Materials:

☐ Documentation and/or Performance Appraisals on hand.

☐ Severance material prepared in writing:

    ☐ Notification letter (working and nonworking notice)

    ☐ Salary continuation/severance period

    ☐ Benefits

    ☐ Life insurance

    ☐ Lump sum settlements

    ☐ Accrued vacation

    ☐ Vested or special pension

    ☐ Savings plan

    ☐ Profit sharing

    ☐ Stock options

    ☐ Bonus

    ☐ Outplacement counseling

    ☐ Automobile

☐ Other resources:

    ☐ Secretarial support

    ☐ Copier/typing services

    ☐ Phone answering

Prepare Message:

☐ Script prepared in writing.

☐ Announcement to remaining employees prepared.

Arrange Next Steps:

☐ Additional scheduled meetings:
HR/Personnel/Outplacement

☐ Prepare yourself emotionally:

    ☐ Employee's reactions anticipated and
responses prepared.

    ☐ Manager's feelings acknowledged and
discussed.

Conducting the Termination Meeting

3

To a large extent the success of the termination meeting will depend upon your thoroughness in documenting and preparing the information and logistics as outlined in the previous chapters. Also of great importance is your ability to communicate information in a way that balances the personal needs of the Employee and the facts of the situation. The final element of success will be your ability to listen to the Employee, allowing him/her to vent emotions and feelings, while managing your own emotions and reactions.

Communication Guidelines

Invite the Employee to sit down.

Avoid small talk, get right to the point, and communicate the decision within the first five minutes of the meeting.

The termination meeting should not extend beyond 10-15 minutes. Once the Employee indicates interest in the next step, move on; do not keep talking.

Don't get defensive.

Be prepared to listen.

Briefly describe the reasons for the decision; be factual.

Explain that there is no open position for the individual and give the reasons.

Advise the Employee that the decision has been reviewed and is final; do not debate.

Give the Employee the notification letter.

Review the important information:

> Notice period (working and nonworking notice).
> Salary continuation period.
> Benefit status.
> Outplacement counseling (if appropriate).

Provide an opportunity for the Employee to ask questions.

Discuss the logistics of the Employee's transition:

> Work flow.
> Departure from work area.
> Security check-out.

Structure next steps:

> Inform Employee of next appointment (Human Resources, Personnel or Outplacement Counselor).
>
> Be sure that Employee understands schedule/ responsibilities for remainder of work time.
>
> Ask for and respond to questions; listen, don't argue.
>
> Arrange for, or maintain, ongoing follow-up.
>
> Close the meeting and escort the Employee to next appointment.

Managing Employee Reactions

Once you have delivered the essence of the termination notice (first five minutes of the meeting), you will focus on managing the Employee's reactions. If you have tried to anticipate reactions and have practiced responses, you will be more comfortable and skilled in dealing with the

16

actual situation. If possible, practice with representatives from the Human Resources Department or your outplacement professional.

Individuals behave in a variety of ways when under stress. Some employees may not display any unusual emotions or reactions; they may realistically accept the facts of the situation. In the case of an individual termination for performance reasons, it is likely that previous discussions have alerted and prepared the Employee to face the possibility of termination. In some instances, however, employees may exhibit extremes of emotion.

Cues for recognizing various reactions and suggestions for dealing with them are outlined below:

Anger: The angry person often becomes challenging; he/she may verbally attack the Manager and say negative things about the company.

> Remain calm; don't get defensive.
>
> Don't argue or threaten.
>
> Don't personalize the anger.
>
> Let the Employee vent.
>
> Use restatement and silence.
>
> Don't feel you have to control the Employee's reaction.
>
> Acknowledge that you hear what is being said.
>
> Focus your comments on the script that you prepared in advance.
>
> Move to the next steps when the Employee provides an opportunity.

Shock: The shocked individual often does not seem to react. Shock is characterized by the individual's silence and staring expression when confronted with the news of termination.

> Use silence and open-ended questions.

Give the Employee time to internalize the message; don't overload him/her with information.

Allow the Employee to express emotion.

Provide support and structure by outlining next steps.

Bring the meeting to closure and move the Employee to other scheduled appointments and additional emotional support.

Denial/Control: The individual who reacts this way is likely to imply that he/she has anticipated the news and is prepared. The intent is to appear as if everything is under control, when in fact, he/she is denying reality.

Make sure the Employee understands the message; if necessary, repeat or restate the information.

Listen actively and ask questions to confirm that your message is being understood by the Employee.

Ask the Employee to restate the information.

Don't try to help the Employee "process" or work through the emotions; you may not have the time or expertise to deal effectively with their reactions. Inform Personnel, Human Resources, or Outplacement Counselors about the reaction.

Move on to the "next steps" in the process.

Regardless of the Employee's reaction, the role of the terminating Manager is well defined:

Rely upon the written documentation or rationale that you have prepared in advance of the meeting.

Reduce the Employee's anxiety by providing structure.

Do not attempt to draw out the Employee's feelings or emotions. Your role is to deliver the notice, listen, answer questions, and move the Employee to the "next step." If the company is providing Outplacement Counseling, the Employee will have skilled professionals to assist him/her in dealing with the emotions that follow termination.

DOs for Conducting the Termination Meeting

☐ Do invite the Employee to sit down

☐ Do get right to the point

☐ Do explain the actions taken and the reasons

☐ Do listen to the Employee and wait for a response

☐ Do restate the message if necessary

☐ Do use your prepared notes/guidelines

☐ Do clarify the separation date

☐ Do give an overview of the separation package

☐ Do explain the logistics for leaving the company

☐ Do provide appropriate written materials

☐ Do close the meeting within 15 minutes

☐ Do escort the Employee to the next appointment

DON'Ts for Conducting the Termination Meeting

- ☐ Don't say, "Good Morning," "Good to see you," or, "How are you?"
- ☐ Don't engage in small talk
- ☐ Don't use humor
- ☐ Don't be apologetic
- ☐ Don't defend, justify, or argue
- ☐ Don't threaten
- ☐ Don't discuss other employees
- ☐ Don't sympathize
- ☐ Don't try to minimize the situation
- ☐ Don't make promises
- ☐ Don't personalize the anger
- ☐ Don't make personal attacks on the individual or organization
- ☐ Don't deviate from your script/notes
- ☐ Don't use platitudes like, "I know how you feel," or,"You will be just fine," etc.

Checklist for Conducting the Termination Meeting

Use the following outline as a "script" for conducting the meeting and to help you prepare for the discussion.

☐ **Briefly describe the decision and the reasons for it.**

☐ **Specify the Employee's separation date.**

☐ **Explain why the Employee was identified for termination.**

☐ **State that the decision has been reviewed and is final.**

☐ **Give the Employee his/her notification letter and review:**

    ☐ Length of notice: working/nonworking

    ☐ Salary continuation/severance

    ☐ Benefits

    ☐ Outplacement

    ☐ Other

☐ **Listen to the Employee, but do not indicate any willingness to reverse the decision.**

☐ **Review the logistics of the transition:**

    ☐ Transfer of projects

    ☐ Clearing of office

    ☐ Security check-out

    ☐ Immediate next steps

☐ **Respond appropriately to the Employee's reaction.**

☐ **Rely upon the written documentation or rationale that you have prepared in advance of the meeting.**

Group Terminations

4

Company efforts to streamline operations often result in large-scale reductions in the workforce...group terminations. Under such circumstances, the psychological bond that traditionally unites employer and employee is severed. As people lose their jobs, remaining employees lose confidence. The company struggles with productivity, morale, legal and public image issues. Confusion and insecurity replace the stability and direction of the past.

In the midst of this environment is you, the Manager, who is responsible not only for carrying out the termination strategy, but also for managing the "survivors." Your role is complicated by your own feelings and emotions.

As in the case of individual terminations, logistics must be coordinated, materials prepared, and next steps arranged. In addition, senior management must consider the following questions in order to develop a communication plan that will guide the termination process:

What is the message?

Who will communicate the message–
>   Senior management? Human Resources/Personnel
>   Department? Department manager? Other?

How will the information be conveyed to those who are being terminated–
>   One-on-one meetings? Group meetings?
>   When, where?

How will the message be communicated to "survivors"–
  Individual or work group meetings?
  Agenda for work group meetings?

Communicating the message is complicated by the fact that it is often the "good worker" whose job is eliminated. The role of the Manager shifts from documenting the performance problem to explaining the company rationale and the business strategy behind the decision to terminate competent employees.

The scope of the restructuring, the culture of the company, and the resources available will dictate how information will be conveyed to those who are terminated. Whether the message is delivered in a series of individual meetings or in a group setting, it is crucial to minimize anxiety and confusion by delivering the message consistently, and by being extremely well organized logistically.

Regardless of who communicates the message or how the information is conveyed, both the terminated and remaining employees will look to you, the Manager, for leadership, guidance, and support. Throughout the termination process, it is important to:

Be visible: This applies throughout the termination day, but especially immediately after the termination discussions.

Show empathy to all employees: Both terminated and remaining employees are entitled to your empathy, discretion, and respect. Avoid making gratuitous remarks and negative comments. Be discreet, honest, and factual in all of your conversations. Remember, humor is inappropriate, even if well intentioned.

Expect emotional comments: Listen and don't become defensive.

Be specific about work tasks: Employees will need a clear sense of direction. Providing specifics and focusing on their responsibilities will add a sense of order to the uncertainty around them.

Provide consistent information: Consistency on your part will enable your employees to trust the information you provide and follow your leadership.

Avoid guessing about unresolved issues: Be honest about what you know and what you don't know. Don't make predictions about the future.

In order to deal effectively with the remaining work group, it is critical that you, as Manager, schedule a meeting as soon after the termination discussions as possible. Remember that in the absence of information, uncertainty and anxiety will increase. Rumors abound. By meeting with your work group you can reduce the level of uncertainty. By dealing openly and honestly with retained employees, you can help to rebuild morale, maintain productivity, and move beyond the confusion and emotion of the moment.

Because of the enormous impact of change, many corporations choose to retain professional Outplacement Counselors and Corporate Revitalization Specialists to assist managers in the process of restructuring the organization. The benefits of such expert advice are numerous. However, in the absence of such assistance, the following tools and resources can be used to facilitate the process.

Special Note: Voluntary Separations: Many companies today are implementing voluntary separation programs. All employees or certain identified groups are given incentives such as increased severance or early retirement benefits if they voluntarily leave the company. Such voluntary separation programs often decrease the need for involuntary terminations or eliminate them altogether.

You may be called on to help administer a voluntary separation program or explain it to employees. While such a program may appear to be less traumatic and stressful than an involuntary termination, be aware that many of the same issues and emotions surface among the affected employees. Be prepared to deal with these emotions, and familiarize yourself with the basic provisions of the voluntary separation package so you can explain their impact to each affected employee. You may want to refer the employees to Human Resources for a more detailed examination of his or her specific situation and separation package.

Structure for Work Group Meetings

- ☐ **Schedule the meeting (within one hour of the terminations).**

- ☐ **Communicate accurately:**

    - ☐ State the reasons for the terminations.

    - ☐ Explain the company's new direction.

    - ☐ Explain changes in structure, goals, priorities.

    - ☐ Explain department plan.

- ☐ **Be direct and honest about unresolved issues.**

- ☐ **Solicit and listen to employee concerns.**

- ☐ **Arrange follow-up meetings:**

    - ☐ Group goals and responsibilities.

    - ☐ Individual performance and career objectives.

- ☐ **Provide structure:**

    - ☐ Outline specific expectations.

- ☐ **Close the meeting:**

    - ☐ Emphasize your availability.

- ☐ **Do not discuss employee reaction with others.**

Summary

The process of change is both necessary and painful. Its effect is pervasive, touching all parts of our personal and work lives. To survive and thrive amid change, both individuals and organizations must develop coping strategies. To some extent, professional success and personal growth are measured by the way we meet the demands of change.

As a Manager, you are an agent for change. This booklet has focused on one dimension of that role–the responsibility for managing and communicating termination information. The degree to which you accept and carry out that role will correspondingly influence individual lives and organizational performance. The professional skill and concern that you demonstrate during the termination interview will characterize you and your organization positively in the minds of both terminated and retained employees. The advice and guidelines presented in this booklet provide you the opportunity to respond in a humane way to a difficult business decision. When all is said and done, that is the bottom line.

Common Reactions and Suggested Responses

Providing correct and consistent responses to reactions and statements made by terminated employees is extremely important. If you are unsure of answers relating to benefits, salary continuation, unemployment compensation, or similar areas, refer the Employee to the appropriate Human Resources specialist. DBM generally encourages you not to be the expert on anything other than the reason why a person is being terminated. Discussion of benefits should be left to those who are authorities on the topic. This also provides for another level of ventilation that is very necessary for the terminated individual.

The reactions and responses below are general examples of how others have dealt effectively with these issues during a termination discussion. The responses that you prepare need to reflect the specific policies of your company and may therefore differ slightly from what follows.

Why was I selected? Who made the final decision? On what basis was the evaluation made?

The selection was based on a number of factors, including individual job skills, work experience, organizational needs, tenure, and performance. These decisions are always difficult, but they were reviewed and approved by management.

What recourse do I have?

Employees are always free to talk with a higher level of management. However, because all of the decisions have been carefully reviewed by management, it is unlikely that the outcome will change.

Can I continue to work for a period of time?

No. We feel it is in your best interest and the company's that you utilize your time exploring employment opportunities outside the company. That is also why we have brought in a special firm to assist you in preparing for your job search.

Can I be rehired?

You are eligible for rehire. However, the probability of that happening is unlikely. That is why you should concentrate your efforts on finding employment outside the company.

How will you handle my references?

By policy, the company limits release of personal information to external requesters. The Human Resources Department will provide potential new employers with dates of employment and job titles.

I want to talk with Mr./Ms. "X" (the Manager's boss).

Of course you are free to make an appointment to see him/her, but I must tell you that he/she is fully aware of the decision and supports it.

In an organization this large, I can't understand why I can't be considered for something else.

Before this decision was made, every effort was made to explore other options.

I don't want to talk about this without my lawyer present.

You are, of course, free to have a legal representative contact us. However, our present commitment is to help you get reestablished as quickly as possible in something that makes sense for you with the least disruption to that makes sense for you with the least disruption to your career and personal life. We strongly suggest that you keep your appointment with the Human Resources representatives and your Outplacement Counselor.

(If a lawyer contacts you, refer the attorney to your company's legal counsel. Do not engage in any conversation.)

How can you do this to me after "X" years?

This reorganization was necessary for business reasons.

You're not going to get away with this. I'm going to get even with you!

I'm sorry you feel that strongly, but I want to reemphasize that we are committed to helping you reestablish yourself in a new position as quickly as possible. I strongly urge you, regardless of your feelings now, to keep the appointment with your Outplacement Counselor.

Was John Smith let go?

I'm not going to answer any questions about other employees. I know you would want the same consideration extended to you.

Will you personally assist me? After all, you are my boss!

The company has provided a comprehensive support package that will be available to you.

Manager Guidelines

Should this person be terminated?

Have all possibilities been exhausted?

Is appropriate documentation available?

Does the person know he/she is not performing up to expectations?

What are the possible legal risks?

Discrimination on account of age, sex, race, religion, national origin, or handicap could be charged by any "protected employee."

Contractual obligations that are either expressed or implied by employee handbook, employee enrollment documents, etc.

What will be the reason given for the termination?

Who is to conduct the termination? When? Where?

If performance is the issue:

> Relate to business situation, including economic pressures, need to reduce total staffing, elimination of the position.

> Have on record objective appraisals of performance (preferably two written and acknowledged appraisals);

they should not be ambiguous, last minute, or contain discriminatory language. In group situations, if performance appraisal systems are weak, forced ranking can be used where you have to select the poor performer based on department/company-wide criteria.

What do you plan to have with you during the termination?

Fact sheet on the individual.

Separation package written out.

Emergency numbers.

What are the possible emotional reactions you might expect from the Terminee?

Does he/she expect to be terminated?

How will he/she take it?

What emotional reactions are likely?

Any physical or medical problems?

Any indication of neurotic or pathological behavior?

How do you plan to deal with trauma or emotional reactions?

Outline ahead of time the points you want to cover.

Arrange for privacy with no interruptions.

Have medical aid on hand if it seems advisable.

Have OPC counselor nearby.

OK to have a "personnel aide" if you wish.

Avoid "getting hooked" into arguments or upset feelings.

Be mentally prepared for a variety of feelings and reactions on both sides.

Defer detailed discussion until later.

Express understanding of upset feelings, but avoid sympathy and platitudes.

If things become too emotional, recess and continue later.

How do you plan to deal with the "why me?" or, "why now?"

Tell the Terminee that this is a business decision and not a personal one.

How do you plan to deal with the termination package?

Clarify how/when duties end.

Clarify the financial package:

> Salary continuation until...
> Benefit continuation until...
> Life insurance.
> Lump sum settlements.
> Accrued vacation.
> Vested or special pension.
> Savings plan.
> Profit sharing.
> Stock options.
> Bonus.
> Automobile.

When and how to recover credit cards, company car, office keys, manuals, etc.

Other resources available:

> Use of secretary.
> Copier, typing help.
> Phone answering services.
> Use of credit cards for job search.

Expect to file for unemployment compensation?

Where "terminee" can go for clarification and help concerning benefits.

How will expense accounts and advances be settled up?

How do you plan to discuss outplacement counseling?

Highly professional assistance on how to go about the process of finding the right job.

Fees and expenses paid by the company.

Let DBM consultant explain how it works.

DBM is not "going to find him/her a job."

How long do you plan for the termination to take?

Be brief and factual about the decision you have made, and put it in a business context.

Minimize small talk and "circling."

Total time target —15 minutes.

What is employee expected to do immediately after termination?

How is the Employee to sort out and remove personal belongings while minimizing embarrassment?

What will be the future access to the premises?

Where is Employee expected to go immediately after the termination interview?

How do you plan to deal with remaining internal employees?

What will be the official story?

Will there be an announcement? Is it ready?

Who will make the announcement?

To whom? When?

Outplacement Counseling

Definition

Outplacement counseling is simply defined as providing job search assistance to an individual or individuals who have been terminated for whatever reason. The corporation or organization either pays an outside consultant or has the in-house capabilities to provide counseling services to the employees it has displaced.

Why Offer It?

Companies that utilize outplacement counseling services reap significant benefits. First of all, a good outplacement program enables management to make timely decisions on individuals who are not performing. Rather than postpone a decision for fear that the person being considered for termination might be hurt, a good program allows the Manager to feel comfortable with the knowledge that the individual will receive counseling and support. This eliminates the games people play in corporate life of putting individuals on what used to be called "shelves." Shelved careers tend to create blockage throughout the organization and prevent growth.

Outplacement assistance can assure management that someone's career will not be stopped just because he/she did not work out at the current company. In essence, outplacement assistance programs help take the sting out of termination for both the company and the person doing the terminating, as well as for the individual being terminated.

Secondly, an outplacement program greatly reduces the legal risk connected with terminations. For example, if proper assistance programs are provided, a part of those programs can be devoted to determining whether or not the company has good reason for termination. Advanced planning for the termination is part of a good outplacement process and enables management to uncover potential legal problems it might have in carrying out the termination.

A third major benefit of outplacement assistance is that it helps the individual look to the future–to the new job– rather than concentrate on the loss of the past job. The individual, therefore, begins to think positively about the next position, an attitude which clearly enhances his/her prospects. In addition, a former employee in this frame of mind is far less likely to consider legal action against his/her past company.

A fourth advantage of an outplacement program is that it provides favorable impact on internal morale. Employees feel much better about their company and tend to side with management in terms of the decision if they know that termination is handled fairly. If, on the other hand, employees believe a colleague was treated unfairly or insensitively, they worry about how they would be treated should it ever happen to them.

Along with internal morale, a company today must also consider the factor of public image. Some executives who are terminated end up publishing articles reviewing how badly the company is faring. This type of statement in a major publication can damage the company's image, especially in terms of its ability to recruit on college campuses as well as to retain top management within the organization. Other individuals who are fired may end up working for competitive or client companies. This can be significant if the termination was handled improperly and the former employee spreads the word.

Finally, a good outplacement counseling program can save money for the company by reducing lengthy severance payments. Outplacement counseling can help top level and middle management effectively move more quickly into new positions by teaching them how to gain contacts in executive search firms, corporations, placement agencies, etc., that would be difficult for them to compile on their own. When counseled and given direction, people tend to move in a much faster and more decisive way toward their next jobs. This also reduces the time they spend trying to "get back" at the company or individual who did the termination. Outplacement counseling can also reduce the opportunity for legal action so often connected with termination.

Where Is Outplacement Today?

Years ago, career assistance programs were virtually unheard of. At best, a personnel generalist would try to counsel his or her friend who was adversely affected by a termination. By now, most of the Fortune 1000 corporations have utilized some form of outplacement counseling. The degree and type of counseling offered to employees varies according to the situation, but most companies provide some assistance to all displaced individuals. Usually higher level employees receive individual service, while nonexempt and hourly employees are often provided with assistance in group settings.

Statistics

Drake Beam Morin, Inc. provides support to help an individual run an efficient, well-researched job search campaign. Of course, industry and job market trends, as well as seasonality, affect how quickly an individual is placed, as does the level of commitment the individual has to the job search.

Approximately 15 percent of Drake Beam Morin's counselees change careers entirely, going from industry to nonprofit/educational organizations or into their own businesses. The large majority, however, stay in the field in which they are working.

It is extremely important for outplacement support services to provide career path counseling to reduce what we call the "bounce rate." Many individuals who are terminated after many years with a company have a tendency to go out, find a job, and experience difficulties in the new position. They then bounce from that job into another, often repeating this pattern for a number of years. This usually happens because the terminated employees did not take time to ascertain why they were terminated or to honestly determine the proper work environment or career path within which they would be successful in the future.

Finding a job is not a statistical endeavor. Nonetheless, some interesting statistics are: about 70 percent of out-placed individuals find jobs through networking personal contacts; about 20 percent find jobs through executive search and placement agencies; and about 10 percent find jobs through mailing letters, answering ads, etc. The utilization of individual contacts produces the best results for finding a position in today's managerial world.

These statistics have held constant for over 25 years of DBM's history. We conduct several surveys each year that review job search methods, and networking is still the number one way to find a new job.

Questions to Ask When Selecting an Outplacement Firm

Resources

How many professional staff members are there?

What are their backgrounds and credentials?

How many clients are served each year?

How many offices does the firm have and are they wholly owned?

What is the quality and atmosphere of the office space?

How sophisticated and available are the secretarial and support services?

How are fees structured and what, exactly, do they include?

What is the overall reputation of the firm?

Unique Services

Does the firm have any special resources for actually linking clients to the job market?

Is the firm able to provide counseling to individuals who want to start or buy their own business?

Is any assistance provided to managers who must terminate an employee?

Are senior executives handled differently than middle managers?

Does the firm provide any programs for candidates' spouses?

What resources are available to a client conducting a national or international job search (office network, support services, consulting resources)?

Commitment to Excellence

How are the professional staff members trained?

What are the ongoing development activities?

What happens if a client is placed and loses his/her job again within a year?

How often does the firm provide feedback to the sponsor company and in what format?

What new techniques or approaches has the firm pioneered in the field of outplacement and career management?

Suggested Reading: Organizational Change and the Consulting Process

Belasco, James. *Teaching the Elephant to Dance.* New York: Plume, 1991.

Beckhard, Richard, and Reuben Harris. *Organizational Transitions: Managing Complex Change.* Reading, MA: Addison-Wesley, 1987.

Graham, Axel R. *Handbook of Employee Termination.* New York: Wiley, 1991.

Guy, Mary E. *From Organizational Decline To Organizational Renewal.* Westport, CT: Quorum, 1989.

Hornstein, Harvey A. *Managerial Courage: Revitalizing Your Company Without Sacrificing Your Job.* New York: Wiley, 1986.

Kanter, Rosabeth. *When Giants Learn To Dance.* New York: Simon & Schuster, 1989.

Kilmann, Ralph H., Teresa Joyce Covin, et al. *Corporate Transformation.* San Francisco: Jossey-Bass, 1989.

Kirkpatrick, Donald L. *How To Manage Change Effectively.* San Francisco: Jossey-Bass, 1988.

Kissler, Gary. *The Change Riders: Managing the Power of Change.* Reading, MA: Addison-Wesley, 1991.

Lippitt, Gordon L., Peter Lanseth, and Jack Mossop. *Implementing Organizational Change.* San Francisco: Jossey-Bass, 1986.

Morin, William J., and James C. Cabrera. *Parting Company: How to Survive the Loss of a Job and Find Another Successfully.* New York: Harcourt Brace Jovanovich, 1991.

Morton, Michael S. *The Corporation of the 1990's.* New York: Oxford University Press, 1991.

Nora, John C., Raymond Rogers, and Robert Stramy. *Transforming The Work Place.* Princeton, NJ: Princeton Research Press, 1986.

Rock, Milton L. and Robert H. *Corporate Restructuring.* New York: McGraw-Hill, 1990.

Srivastva, Suresh, Ronald Fry and Associates. *Executive and Organizational Continuity.* San Francisco: Jossey-Bass, 1992.

Tichy, Noel M., and Mary Anne Devanna. *The Transformational Leader.* New York: Wiley, 1990.

Tomasko, Robert M. *Downsizing: Reshaping the Corporation for the Future.* New York: AMACOM, 1990.

Tylczak, Lynn. *Downsizing Without Disaster.* Los Altos, CA: Crisp Publications, 1991.

About Drake Beam Morin, Inc.

Drake Beam Morin, Inc. (DBM) is the world's leading human resource management consulting firm. DBM provides organizations and their employees with the highest caliber services and products available in the areas of employee selection, performance and transition management.

Established in 1967, we have assisted more than 50,000 organizations of all types and sizes and over a million individuals at all employee levels. The wealth of experience, which far surpasses any other firm in the industry, enables DBM to offer organizations the expertise that most effectively and efficiently meets their human resource challenges.

Through a network of over 150 locations around the globe, DBM provides personalized attention on a local level, along with a vast array of resources, wherever you may be located. With DBM, you have the best of two worlds: a local firm with a global presence.

To find out more about how any of DBM's programs can benefit your organization, contact your local DBM office or Marketing Services, DBM Corporate Headquarters, 100 Park Avenue, New York NY 10017 Telephone 212 692-5813.

To receive our free products catalog, write or call DBM Publishing, 100 Park Avenue, New York NY 10017 Telephone 800 345-JOBS.

About the Author

William J. Morin is Chairman and CEO of Drake Beam Morin, Inc., the world's largest human resource management consulting firm. Mr. Morin's innovative solutions and approaches to the ever-changing challenges of Human Resource Management have earned him a worldwide reputation as an industry leader.

Terminated once himself, Mr. Morin is well aware of the need for managers to understand the nuances of the termination process in order to effectively, and sensitively, handle terminations.

In his role as CEO, Mr. Morin consults with major companies facing corporate restructuring and reorganizations.

In addition to this book, Mr. Morin has co-authored *Parting Company: How to Survive the Loss of a Job and Find Another Successfully* with James C. Cabrera and *Dismissal: There is no easy way but there is a better way* with Lyle Yorks. He has also written a book on corporate loyalty titled *Trust Me.*